Hustling and Bustling
ROCKETS

WHEELS AND AUTOMOBILES

FOX EYE
PUBLISHING

Earth

space ——

A rocket is a spectacular spacecraft that blasts off and shoots through the sky.

Moon

Up and up into space it goes. Off to the Moon it flies.

Rockets have rocket engines.
The engines set the fuel on fire.

Fuel turns into hot gas and shoots out the back.
This pushes the rocket higher.

parachute

rocket booster

On each side is a rocket booster.
They blast the rocket up off the ground.

When the rocket is up, the boosters are dropped and they parachute back down.

fuel tank

The fuel tank pushes the rocket higher by burning liquid fuel.

Now, the rocket is nearly in space.
It drops its fuel tank, too.

The rocket shakes and shudders as it moves through Earth's atmosphere.

The rocket is moving very fast, and space is getting near!

atmosphere

The sky changes from blue to black as the
rocket leaves Earth's atmosphere.

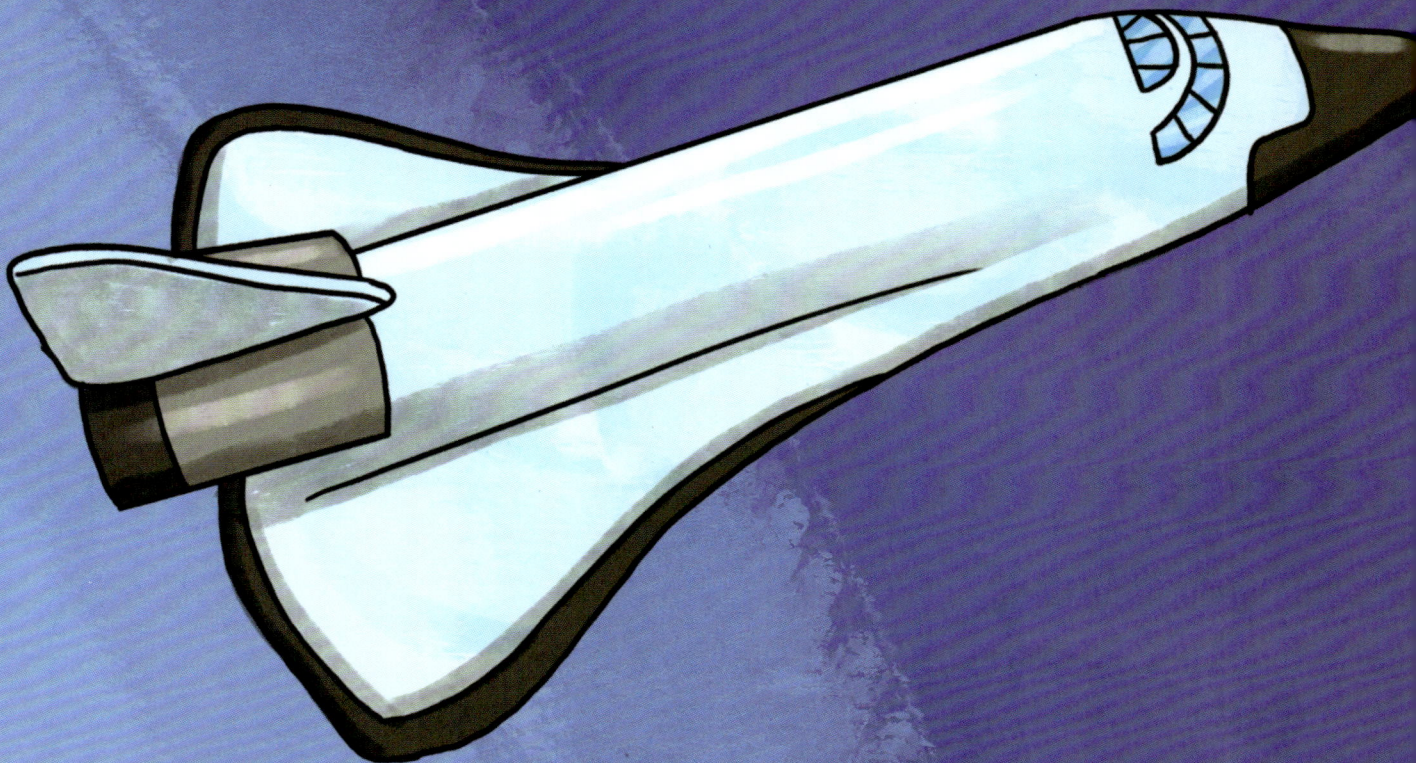

The rocket glides along smoothly now.
Here the stars shine bright and clear.

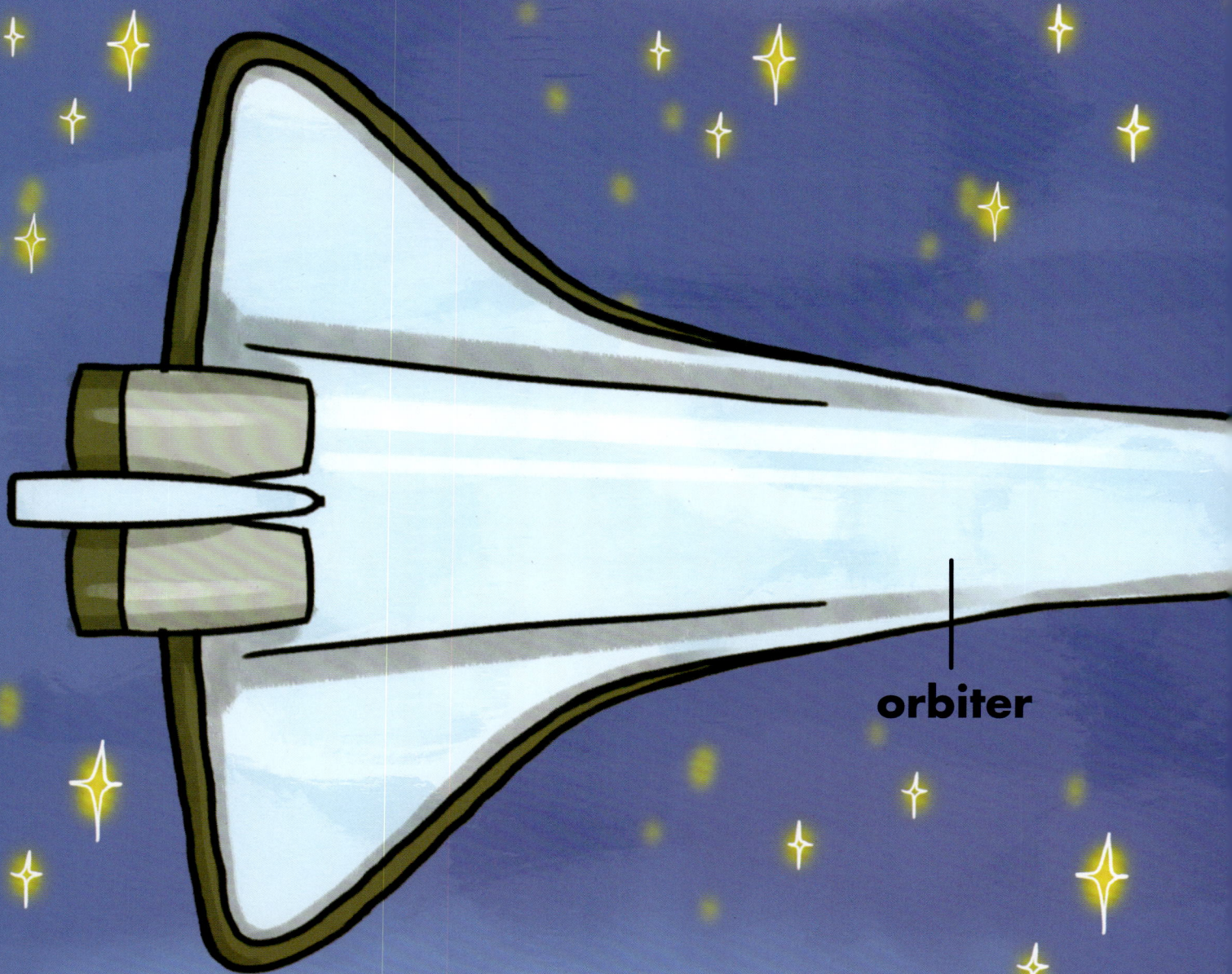

orbiter

The rocket has an orbiter.
The engines steer it left and right.

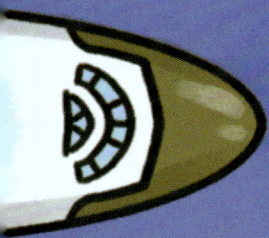

The orbiter flies in space like a
plane. The astronauts travel inside.

Moon

In space, the astronauts float in the air.
Their food floats, too. And so does their hair!

Earth

The orbiter travels around the Moon.
From space, Earth is a beautiful blue.

galaxies

In space, there are wonderful things to see.
There are other planets and galaxies.

Some galaxies spread out. Some spiral around.
The Milky Way is where Earth is found.

drag chute

Now, it is time to go home. Earth is near.
The orbiter enters the atmosphere.

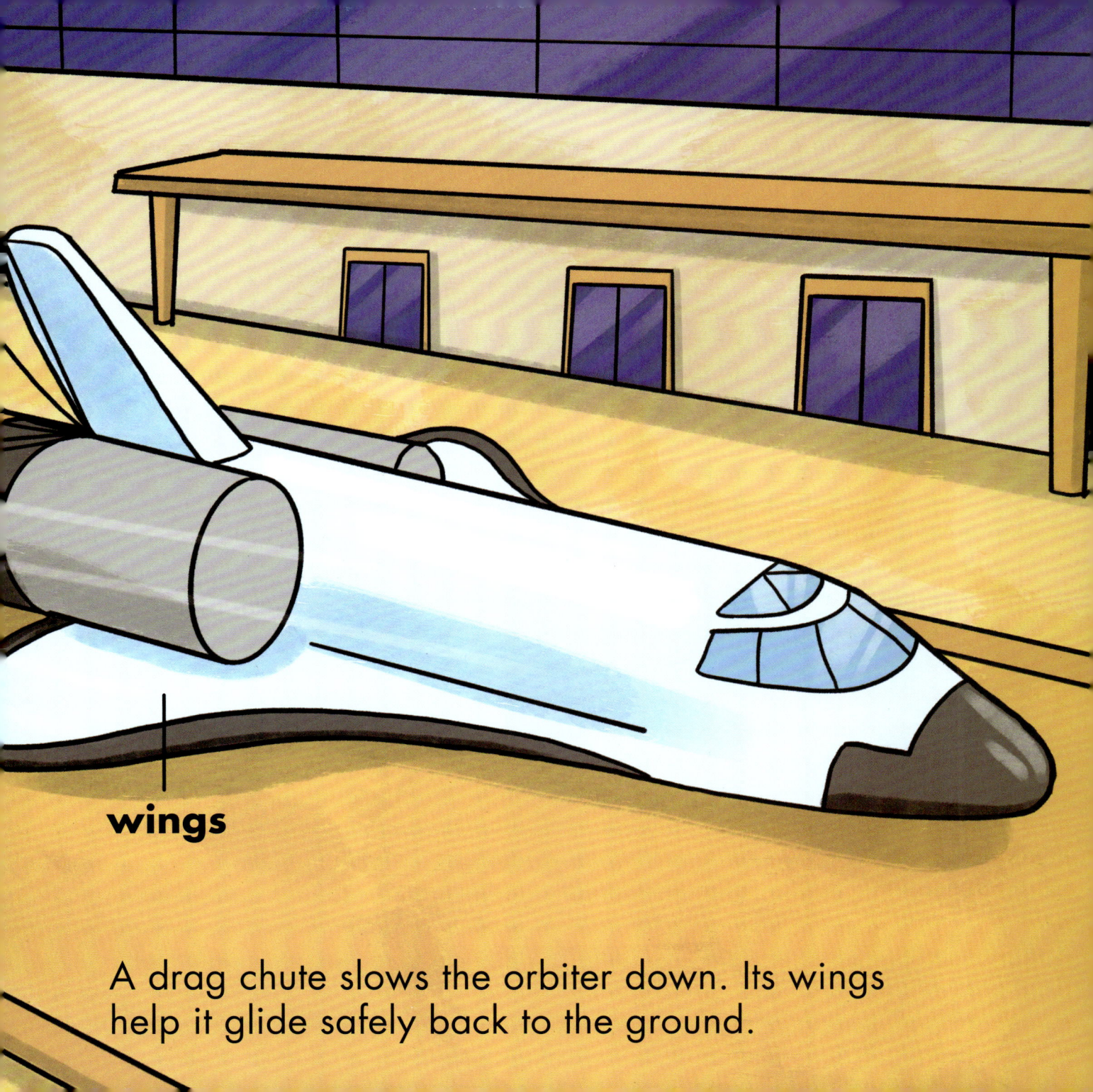

wings

A drag chute slows the orbiter down. Its wings help it glide safely back to the ground.

Bustling Words

Astronauts are people who travel into space.

The **atmosphere** what we call the many gases around Earth.

Blasts off means to leave Earth and go into space.

A **drag chute** is like a parachute, or a piece of material that slows down something as it flies.

Engines are parts of rockets that make their energy.

Fuel is energy that machines need to make them work.

A **fuel tank** stores fuel.

A **galaxy** is a group of millions of stars.

A **machine** is something that helps us to do work.

An **orbiter** is part of a space vehicle that carries astronauts.

A **parachute** is a piece of material that slows down something as it flies.

A **rocket booster** is part of a rocket that passes fuel to the engines.

Steer means to move left, right, up or down.

The Milky Way is the galaxy where Earth, the Sun, and the Moon are.

First published in 2024 by Fox Eye Publishing
Unit 31, Vulcan House Business Centre,
Vulcan Road, Leicester, LE5 3EF
www.foxeyepublishing.com

Author: Katherine Eason
Art director: Paul Phillips
Cover designer: Emma Bailey
Editor: Jenny Rush

All illustrations by Eszter Szepvolgyi

978-1-80445-342-1

Printed in China